Holdstein

EDIT!

TOM WALDREP
University of South Carolina
Computer Assisted Language Learning, Inc.

ROBERT OAKMAN
University of South Carolina
Computer Assisted Language Learning, Inc.

COLLIN BAKER
Computer Assisted Language Learning, Inc.

McGraw-Hil, Inc.
New York   St. Louis   San Francisco   Auckland   Bogotá
Caracas   Hamburg   Lisbon   London   Madrid   Mexico
Milan   Montreal   New Delhi   Paris   San Juan
São Paulo   Singapore   Sydney   Tokyo   Toronto

This book was developed by STEVEN PENSINGER, Inc.

EDIT!

Copyright © 1990 by McGraw-Hill, Inc. All rights reserved. Printed in the United States of America. Except as permitted under the United States Copyright Act of 1976, no part of this publication may be reproduced or distributed in any form or by any means, or stored in a data base or retrieval system, without the prior written permission of the publisher.

1 2 3 4 5 6 7 8 9 0 DSI DSI 9 5 4 3 2 1 0

P/N 540956-9

The editor was Steve Pensinger;
the production supervisor was Anthony DiBartolomeo.
Distribution Systems, Inc. was printer and binder.

About Edit!

Edit! is a computerized program designed specifically to be used in English writing classes, in the writing laboratory, or on home computers. The program runs on IBM-compatible personal computers with a minimum of 256K of memory and version 2.0 (or higher) of the PC-DOS or MS-DOS operating system.

Edit!...

— enables you to focus your writing style and method of presentation to fit the needs of the assignment. The program asks you to consider the audience, purpose, format, and style requirements of your work at both the pre-writing and post-writing stages of its development.

— allows you to prepare the text using the program's word processor. If you already have written materials prepared with other, more sophisticated word processing packages, you may bring them into **Edit!** and perform its special functions on them.

— offers a large variety of editing checks to highlight aspects of your work that may need revision. The heart of the **Edit!** program is its extensive checking of written text on four levels of prose structure: Word, Sentence, Paragraph, and Overall Paper. For example, you will be able to locate and revise slang words or cliches, sexist language, and vague or confusing phrasing in your writing.

— allows you both to check your writing and to revise it without leaving the editing phase of the program. Giving you, the writer, the capabililty to edit your text at the moment you decide to make the change discovered by the program checks is one of the significant improvements of **Edit!** over other computer-editing aids.

The levels of the **Edit!** program are independent of each other. You are the writer and the user, and you are in control of what you do with the program. You can run as many or as few of the checks at a sitting as you wish. Because the program has such a large and comprehensive set of writing checks, you may find yourself running it several different times on the same piece of writing before completing your final draft. **Edit!** also provides several options for printing your completed work and storing it on your own disk.

In classroom testing we have found that **Edit!** improves significantly the clarity, vigor, and effectiveness of student's writing. The program has been designed to make use of your judgement in revising and editing you work. We think you will find it a useful guide to better writing.

Table of Contents

Introduction	1
What You Need To Use Edit!	2
Getting Started	2
Installing Edit! on a Hard Disk	4
An Overview of Edit!	4
Keyboard Guide	8
Creating a Document	13
Editing a Document	17
Checking a Document	20
Saving a Document	38
Changing Document Files	38
Printing a Document	39
Changing the Directory	39
Returning Temporarily to DOS	40
Changing the Edit! Setup	40
Quitting Edit!	44

USER'S GUIDE

INTRODUCTION

Edit! is designed especially for use in English writing classes, in the writing laboratory, or at home. It can add to the vigor, clarity, and effectiveness of your writing by helping you to rid it of grammatical errors, cliches, wordiness, and other problems. It also helps you focus your writing to suit a particular purpose or audience.

The heart of Edit! is its checking feature. This feature helps you to improve documents by spotting problems with their grammar, word usage, punctuation, and structure as well as with the development of the ideas they express. The capabilities of the Edit! far exceed those of the dictionaries and thesauruses built into sophisticated word processing systems.

Although its primary usefulness is for checking and editing documents created with full-featured word processing systems, you can also use Edit! to create documents. It includes many — but not all — of the features found in expensive word processing systems. You can insert or delete text with Edit!, for example, and you can center a line or use bold type. You can also search a document for a word, and you can delete large blocks of text with a few keystrokes.

The checking feature of Edit! not only points out possible problems in documents but also offers tips on how to resolve them. You can check a document on four levels: for problems with words, sentences, paragraphs, or the overall document. At each level, you can check for several specific kinds of problems. For example, at the sentence level, you can check for incomplete sentences, sentences that are too long or too short, subject- verb agreement, and misuse of indefinite pronouns. While checking for any type of writing problem, you can display a tutorial screen that provides helpful information about how to avoid it. When using the checking feature, you can suspend it temporarily to edit your work, then resume checking. There's no need to keep notes on paper or to switch continually between the computer screen and a paper copy of the document. You can check the document on any level as many times as you want, printing it only when it meets your highest standards.

WHAT YOU NEED TO USE EDIT!

To use Edit!, you must have:
- an IBM™ PC, PC/XT, PC/AT, or PS/2 computer or one that is fully compatible with any of these
  - at least 256 kilobytes of random access memory
  - PC-DOS or MS-DOS, version 2.0 or higher
- two floppy disk drives or one hard disk drive and one floppy disk drive

GETTING STARTED

Floppy-Disk Systems

Follow these steps each time you use Edit! if your system has two floppy disk drives:

1. Insert the DOS disk in drive A.

2. In drive B, insert the disk on which you will store your documents.

3. Turn on the computer or, if it is already turned on, reset it by holding down the [CTRL] + [ALT] keys and pressing the [DELETE] key.

4. If you see a prompt asking you for the date, type the current date and press [ENTER].

5. If a prompt asks for the time, type the current time and press [ENTER]. You then see the prompt A>.

6. Remove the DOS disk from drive A and replace it with the Edit! disk.

7. If you have a graphics monitor, type **Edit** and press [ENTER]. Or, if you have a monochrome monitor that does not display graphics, type **Edit/s** and press [ENTER].

This will display the Edit! copyright screen, with the software's title in the center and its Main Menu at the bottom.

When you first use Edit!, it is set up to store documents in the primary directory of the floppy disk in drive A.

USER'S GUIDE

Therefore, unless you change the directory setting to store documents on the floppy disk in drive B, Edit! will store your work on the Edit! program disk.

You can change the current directory for a single work session, or you can change the default directory for all work sessions.

For instructions on changing the current directory, turn to the Changing the Directory section (page 39). For instructions on changing the default directory, turn to the Changing the Edit! Setup section and see the Changing the Default Directory heading (page 42).

Hard-Disk Systems

Edit! must first be installed on your hard disk (see hard disk installation instructions on page 4). Then follow these steps each time you use Edit! with a computer that has a hard disk:

1. Turn on the computer.

2. If a prompt asks for the date, type the date and press [ENTER].

3. If a new prompt asks for the time, type the time and press [ENTER].

4.a. If you have installed Edit! on your hard drive, change to the subdirectory containing the program by typing `cd/Edit!` and pressing [ENTER].

-or-

4.b. If you want to run Edit! from your floppy drive, insert the Edit! disk in drive A. At the C prompt, type `A:` and press [ENTER].

7. If you have a graphics monitor, type `Edit` and press [ENTER]. Or, if you have a monochrome monitor that does not display graphics, type `Edit/s` and press [ENTER].

This will display the Edit! copyright screen, with the software's title in the center and its Main Menu at the bottom.

When you first use Edit!, it is set up to store documents

in the primary directory of the floppy disk in drive A. Therefore, unless you change the directory setting to store your work on the hard disk (or on the disk in another floppy disk drive), Edit! will store your work on the Edit! program disk.

You can change the current directory for a single work session, or you can change the default directory for all work sessions.

For instructions on changing the current directory, turn to the Changing the Directory section (page 39). For instructions on changing the default directory, turn to the Changing the Edit! Setup section and see the Changing the Default Directory heading (page 42).

INSTALLING EDIT! ON A HARD DISK

It is easy to copy Edit! onto your hard disk:

1. Start your computer and get to the DOS prompt (usually C:\).

2. Then put your Edit! diskette in the A drive and change to the A drive by typing **A:** and pressing [ENTER].

3. Now type **instedit** and press [ENTER] to create a new subdirectory on your C drive called \Edit! and to copy the necessary Edit! files into it.

You will be asked of it's OK before the program creates the subdirectory. Type a "**y**" and Edit! will be installed automatically; type an "**n**" to stop the installation process. Please note that all the Edit! files must be in the same subdirectory on your hard disk for the program to work properly.

AN OVERVIEW OF EDIT!

Edit! can check and revise documents created with expensive, full-featured word processing programs as well as those you create with Edit! However, any document you create with other software must follow a few simple rules if you are to check it with this program.

USER'S GUIDE

First, you must save your document as an ASCII or DOS text file, which is a type of file that can be used with different kinds of software. Most sophisticated word processing programs can create ASCII files, but some cannot. For instructions on saving the document in an ASCII file, see the manual for the word processing software you used to create the document. In addition, any document you check with Edit! must meet two format requirements: Its paragraphs must be indented four spaces, and two spaces must follow each punctuation mark that ends a sentence. If a document doesn't meet these spacing requirements, adjust the spacing with Edit! or with word processing software before attempting to check the document with Edit! Otherwise, the Edit! checking feature will not work properly.

Check the document first at the **word level**. At this level, Edit! helps you to spot problems with individual words and phrases, such as cliches, slang, and words that are often mistaken for each other. You can also check the document's punctuation at the word level. Next, check the document at the **sentence level**. Here, Edit! helps you to locate and correct problems such as sentence fragments, overly long sentences, and subjects and verbs that don't agree.

When you finish checking and correcting sentences, check the document at the **paragraph level**. At this level, you identify the topic sentence and concluding sentence of each paragraph. You also check for smooth transitions, and you ensure that the pronouns in each paragraph are linked with nouns in the same paragraph.

Finally, check the **overall document**. You can view the topic and concluding sentences to check how well your ideas are developed in the document. You can also check to see that sentence lengths are varied. Edit! can display statistics, such as the average number of words per sentence, that can help you to make a document more readable. It can also display its three post-writing screens: two screens of questions for assessing the effectiveness of your document, and one screen that reminds you of the document's intended audience, purpose, format, and tone.

When you finish checking the document on all levels,

you may need to do more editing. For example, you may want to develop your ideas more fully or smooth the transitions between paragraphs. You can then check the edited document again on any level — as often as you want, until it's perfect. Finally, you can print the document.

Before you exit from Edit! to use another program or turn off the computer, be sure to save the document you have been creating, editing, or checking. You should also save the document from time to time as you write and edit, so you don't lose all your work if the computer is turned off by mistake or accident.

Detailed procedures for using Edit! appear later in subsequent sections of this manual.

Edit! Menus

Using Edit! involves making a series of choices from its menus, which appear at the bottoms of screens. The first menu you see is the Main Menu. It appears at the bottom of the copyright screen when you start Edit!

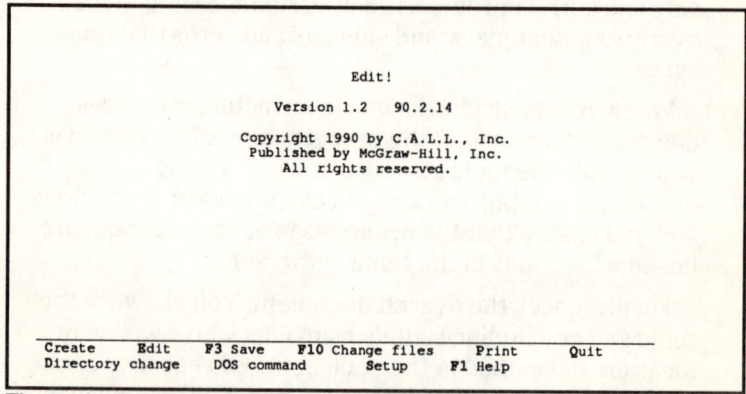

Figure 1 - Copyright Screen with Main Menu

In each option listing on the Main Menu or any other Edit! menu, highlighting indicates which key you press to use the option. On the Main Menu, for example, the C in **Create** is highlighted. To select this option, you press C.

When you select a menu option, Edit! may display a

USER'S GUIDE 7

prompt, which asks for information that Edit! needs before it can proceed. For example, a prompt that appears when you select **Create** from the Main Menu asks for the name of the document you want to create.

Many menu selections lead to other menus. When you select **Edit** from the Main Menu, for example, you see the Create/Edit Menu.

Select the **Check** option from the Create/Edit Menu, and you see the Checking Menu, which includes options that lead to still more menus. (You may see a message before you see the new menu.)

To return to a previous menu, press the [ESCAPE] key. If you are at the Main Menu, [ESCAPE] takes you to the Create/Edit Menu.

The Create/Edit Screen

As you create or edit a document, your work appears on the Create/Edit Screen. Edit! displays this screen after you select **Edit** from the Main Menu. If you have selected **Create,** you see this screen after naming the new document and viewing the pre-write screens. (The pre-write screens are discussed in the Creating a Document section later in this manual.)

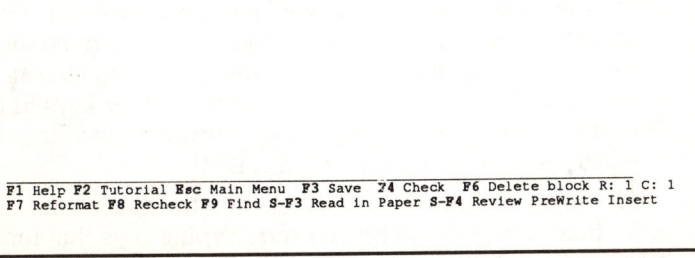

Figure 2 - Create/Edit Screen

The document itself occupies the upper part of the

Create/Edit Screen. If you are creating a document and have not yet begun typing it, or if you are editing a document but have not yet retrieved it from a disk, the upper part of the screen is blank. Menus appear at the bottom of the screen.

At the bottom right corner of the screen is the Insert/Overwrite Indicator. If the indicator says "Insert," the characters on the screen will move to the right, if necessary, to make room for any new characters you type. If the indicator says "Overwrite," the characters you type will replace existing characters.

To switch the indicator between Insert and Overwrite, press the [INSERT] key.

Just above the Insert/Overwrite Indicator is the Cursor Position Indicator. It consists of an R followed by a number and a C followed by another number. It identifies the location of the cursor, which is the point of light that shows where the next character you type will appear. The number after the R identifies the line, or row, on the screen where the cursor is located. The number after the C identifies the column, or the character position in that line. These numbers change continuously as you type and move the cursor.

KEYBOARD GUIDE

To create or revise a document with Edit!, you type in much the same way that you would with a typewriter. Most of the keys on the computer keyboard resemble the keys found on typewriters. A computer keyboard also includes keys for moving the cursor. Several other keys function in different ways with different software, and you need to know how to use them with Edit!

The keys labeled with characters and the space bar work just as they do on typewriters. Typing keys that function somewhat differently on a computer include:

[SHIFT] — You can't lock a shift key to type a series of capital letters, as you do on a typewriter. Instead, press the key labeled [CAPS LOCK]. The [CAPS LOCK] key works the

USER'S GUIDE 9

same way as the shift lock key on a typewriter except that it does not affect the row of number keys above the letter keys. To type the symbols that appear over the numbers on these keys, even if you have already pressed [CAPS LOCK] and are typing capital letters, hold down the [SHIFT] key while pressing the number key. On Edit! menus, shift is abbreviated as S. For example, to select the menu option S-F3 Read in paper, press [SHIFT]-[F3].

[BACKSPACE] — erases any characters in its path as it moves the cursor to the left.

[CR] or [ENTER] — moves the cursor to the beginning of the next line. With Edit!, you don't press [ENTER] at the end of each line as you would with a typewriter. That's because Edit! includes a feature called word-wrap, which automatically moves a word to the next line if it is too long to fit on the line where you begin typing it. However, there are three other situations where you do press [ENTER]:

1. to end a paragraph
2. to leave a line blank
3. to register your response to a prompt. For example, when the system prompts you for the name of a document you are creating, press [ENTER] after typing the name.

The computer keyboard also has keys not found on typewriters. These include keys labeled **Insert, Delete, Escape, Page Down, Page Up, Alt, Control,** and a set of keys labeled **F1, F2,** and so forth.

Control and ALT

Two of these keys, [CTRL] and [ALT], don't do anything by themselves. Like the shift key, they are used in conjunction with other keys. For example, you press [ALT] with the B key before typing text that you want to print bold, then again to resume typing text that you want to print normally. Whenever this manual tells you to use a key combination that includes [ALT] or [CTRL], it will use a hyphen between that key and the other key. Always press these special keys first and hold them down while pressing the other key.

Cursor-Control Keys

Some keys and key combinations are used for moving the cursor around on the screen or for moving from one screen to another. These include:

Arrow keys — [↑], [↓], [←], [→] — The arrow shows the direction the cursor moves in when you press the key. These keys are generally clustered on the right side of the keyboard. Be careful not to confuse these cursor control keys with other keys, such as the backspace key, that may also be labeled with arrows.

To move around the screen more efficiently, you can use the right arrow and left arrow keys in combination with the [CTRL] key. Pressing [CTRL]-[→] moves the cursor to the beginning of the next word. [CTRL]-[←] moves the cursor to the beginning of the current word or, if it's already there, to the beginning of the previous word.

[PAGE DOWN] — This key moves the cursor to the beginning of the next screen of text. [CTRL]-[PAGE DOWN] moves the cursor to the end of the document.

[PAGE UP] — This key is similar to [PAGE DOWN] in reverse. It moves the cursor to beginning of the previous screen of text or, if there is no previous page, to the beginning of the current screen. [CTRL]-[PAGE UP] moves the cursor to the beginning of the document.

[HOME] — This key moves the cursor to the beginning of the line where it's located.

[END] — This key moves the cursor to the end of the line where it's located.

Keys for Deleting Text

Several keys can be used to delete text. They include:

[DELETE] — This key erases the character marked by the cursor.

[BACKSPACE] — This key erases any characters in its path as it moves the cursor to the left.

[CTRL]-[CR] — This key combination deletes all the text from the cursor to the end of the line.

Insert and Overwrite

When you type with Edit!, you use either the insert

USER'S GUIDE 11

feature or the overwrite feature. As you type, the Insert/Overwrite Indicator at the bottom right of the Create/Edit Screen shows which of these features is turned on. When the insert feature is turned on, the existing text moves to the right to make room for the next character you type, and none of the text is erased. If the overwrite feature is turned on instead, the next character you type will replace the character marked by the cursor. To switch between insert and overwrite, press [INSERT].

Function Keys

The function keys, which are labeled **F1**, **F2**, and so on, are used for specialized Edit! features. They are:

[F1] — Press this key to display helpful information about using Edit! The information Edit! displays depends on what is on the screen and what you are doing with it when you press this key. For example, if you press it with the Main Menu on the screen, Edit! displays information about using the Main Menu. If you press this key when you are using the Create/Edit Menu, Edit! provides help with using the keyboard.

[F2] — Press this key to display tutorial information that can help you to use the checking feature of Edit! If you press this key after you begin checking a document, Edit! displays information about the problems for which you are checking.

For example, if you have selected the menu options to check at the word level for slang, pressing this key displays a screen entitled "Help with SLANG, JARGON, AND DIALECT." This screen offers guidelines about the use of this kind of language. If you have not yet selected the type of check you want to make on a document, pressing [F2] lists the four levels of checking and the kinds of checks it can perform on each level.

[F3] — Press this key to save the document you are writing or editing. You can do this when the Create/Edit Menu or the Main Menu appears at the bottom of the screen.

[F4] — Press this key to select the **Check** option from the Create/Edit Menu and use the checking feature of Edit! See the Checking a Document section later in this manual for further instructions on using the **Check** option.

[F5] — While you are checking or editing a document, press this key to unmark a block of text that you have marked with [F6].

[F6] — You can use this key to delete a block of text from a document you are creating or editing. First, move the cursor to the beginning of the block and press this key. Then move the cursor to the end of the block and press it again. Edit! highlights the block you have marked. Press [F6] a third time to delete the highlighted block. To remove the marking from a word, sentence or other block of text, press [F5].

[F7] — If a paragraph includes lines that are too long or too short, position the cursor at the beginning of the paragraph and press this key. Edit! reformats the paragraph to even out the line lengths.

[F8] — While checking a document, press this key to leave the checking feature temporarily so you can correct a problem. Then press it again to resume checking where you left off.

[F9] — To find a word or phrase in a document, move the cursor to the beginning of the document and press this key. Edit prompts you to type the text you want to find. Type the text exactly as it appears in the document, then press [ENTER]. Edit! moves the cursor to the first place in the document where it finds matching text. To find the next place where this text appears in the document, press [F9] and [ENTER].

[SHIFT]-[F2] — To change the right margin while creating or editing a document, press this key combination. When Edit! prompts you for the position of the new right margin, type the new position number and press [ENTER].

[SHIFT]-[F3] — To retrieve a copy of a document from a disk so you can check it or edit it, press this key combination when the Create/Edit Menu is on the screen. Edit! prompts you for the name of the document you want to retrieve. Type the name and press [ENTER]. Edit! then displays the document on the screen.

[SHIFT]-[F4] — Press this key combination to review the prewrite screens for the document you are creating or editing, including the information you typed on Pre-Write Screen 5 about the document's audience, main idea, purpose, format, and tone.

[SHIFT]-[F8] — To center a line of text, position the cursor on the line and press this key combination.

Special Printing Effects

You can create special printing effects with key combinations. These effects will appear on the printed output only; special codes will appear on the computer screen. The key combinations to produce these effects are:

[ALT]-[B] — To print text in bold, press this key combination, type the text, then press [ALT]-[B] again.

[ALT]-[I] — To print text in italic type, press this key combination, type the text, then press [ALT]-[I] again.

[ALT]-[U] — To print text underlined, press this key combination, type the text, then press [ALT]-[U] again.

NOTE: Not all printers can print these special effects.

Returning to an Earlier Menu

To stop what you are doing with Edit! and return to the previous menu, press [ESCAPE]. If the Main Menu is on the screen, this key takes you to the Create/Edit Menu.

CREATING A DOCUMENT

To create a document with Edit!, press C to select **Create** from the Main Menu. Edit! replaces the Main Menu with a prompt asking for the name of the new document.

Naming the Document

You can give the document a name, or you can allow Edit! to name the document WORK.EDT.

To name the document yourself, type a name that includes as many as eight letters or numbers. You can also add a period followed by an extension of up to three letters.

For example, suppose you want to create two papers about symbols for different classes. You could name both papers SYMBOLS and give them different extensions, such as the initials of the class' instructors, to distinguish them from each other. After typing the name and extension, if any, press ENTER.

To use the default name WORK.EDT, press ENTER without typing anything.

If a document by the name you have chosen exists already, Edit! displays a message asking if you want the new document to replace the original.

To keep the original document intact, press the **N** key to return to the Main Menu, then select **Create** again and give the new document a different name. To replace the existing document with the new one, press the **Y** key.

Pre-Write Screens

After you name the new document, Edit! displays the first of its five pre-write screens.

```
                    AUDIENCE                    (Screen 1 of 5)

Your writing will be more effective if you keep in mind who will be reading
your work.  Before you begin to write, know the answers to these questions:

1. Who will be reading what you write?

2. How much do these readers know about your subject already?  Do they know
   the terminology that people knowledgeable about the topic use to discuss
   it?  What prejudices are the readers likely to have about this subject?

3. What do you have in common with your readers that can help you to
   communicate with them more effectively?

4. Is formal language appropriate for your audience, or would an informal
   or conversational tone be more appropriate?

5. Is it appropriate to use personal observations and examples in writing
   for this audience?  If so, what are they?


     PgDn Page down          PgUp Page up       Esc Create/Edit screen
```

Figure 3 - Pre-Write Screen 1

The pre-write screens are designed to help you focus on why you are writing the document and how you can write it most effectively. The first four screens pose questions about the document's audience, purpose, focus, and style. These questions don't require you to type a response;

USER'S GUIDE   15

they are intended to serve as reminders. Pre-Write Screen 5 provides a chart where you can describe the document's audience, purpose, main idea, format, and language. You can refer to the pre-write screens later as you work on the document.

To move from one pre-write screen to the next, you should press [PAGE DOWN]. To move to the preceding pre-write screen, press [PAGE UP].

When you get to Pre-Write Screen 5, press [F3] to begin filling in the chart. Then type a few words on the first line to describe the document's purpose. To go from one line to the next, press [ENTER]. Also press [ENTER] when you finish typing your entry on line four, where you describe the document's tone. You can change your entries on this screen later.

When you finish filling out the chart, or if you don't want to fill it out now, press [ESCAPE] to go to the Create/Edit Screen.

The Create/Edit Screen

When you exit from the pre-write screens, Edit! displays the Create/Edit Screen, which is illustrated on page 7, in the section An Overview of Edit! The Create/Edit Screen is where you type the document. Until you start typing, the Create/Edit Screen has nothing on it except for the Create/Edit Menu, Insert/Overwrite Indicator, and Cursor Position Indicator. As you type, be sure to indent each paragraph four spaces and to leave two spaces after the punctuation at the end of each sentence. Otherwise, the checking feature cannot work properly. The tab key will automatically indent each paragraph the required number of spaces. For more information about how to type a document, turn back to the Keyboard Guide, which begins on page 8.

Saving Your Work

As you type a document, press [F3] to select the **Save** option every few minutes. Then you won't lose all your work if the computer is turned off; you'll lose only what you've done since the last time you used the **Save** option.

When you press [F3], Edit! prompts you for the name of the document file where you want to save your work. The name you typed when you began creating the document is the default name.

To save the document under a different name, type the new name and press [ENTER]. To save the document under the default name, press [ENTER] without typing anything.

When you press [ENTER], Edit! records your work on the storage disk and returns you to where you left off, so you can resume writing the document.

Once you have saved the document, you switch from creating the document to editing it. Should you return to the Main Menu for any reason, you must select **Edit** — not **Create** — to continue working on the document.

Other Create/Edit Menu Options

To check the document for problems with words, sentences, paragraphs, or overall structure, select **Check**. See the Checking a Document section later in this manual for instructions on using this option.

Use the **Reformat** option to adjust line lengths if inserting or deleting text has left some lines too long or too short. To adjust a long or short line as well as the remainder of the paragraph, move the cursor to the start of the line and press [F7].

For instructions on using the **Recheck** option, see the Checking a Document section, which begins on page 20. Use this option only if you have interrupted the checking feature temporarily to make a change in a document.

With the **Find** option, you can search for a word or other group of characters from the cursor location to the end of the document. When you press [F9] to select **Find**, Edit! prompts you to enter the text you want to find.

Type the text exactly as it appears in the document, then press [ENTER]. Edit! highlights the first text in the document that matches what you typed. To find the next place where the same text appears, press [F9] and [ENTER].

You can use the **Read in paper** option to insert a copy of another document in the one you are creating.

To do this, position the cursor where you want the copy to appear and press [SHIFT]-[F3]. Edit! displays a message asking for the name of the document you want to insert. Type the name and press [ENTER], or press [ENTER] without typing anything to insert the default document WORK.EDT.

If you created the document with Edit!, a prompt asks if you want to review the information you filled in on Pre-Write Screen 5. Press **Y** to display this screen or **N** to display the document. Edit! retrieves the document from the storage disk and inserts it in the document you are creating.

Most of the time, however, you won't use the **Read in paper** option when creating a paper. Instead, you will use it to display documents you want to edit.

To review all of the pre-write screens, including what you typed on Pre-Write Screen 5, press [SHIFT]-[F4]. After reviewing the screens, press [ESCAPE] to return to the document.

For information about how to use the keyboard with Edit!, press [F1].

To list the checking levels and the kinds of checks you can make on each level, press [F2].

To return to the Main Menu, press [ESCAPE].

EDITING A DOCUMENT

To edit a document you've already saved on a storage disk, press **E** to select **Edit** from the Main Menu. Edit! displays the Create/Edit Screen, which is illustrated and described in the section An Overview of Edit! earlier in this manual.

If you have not worked on another document since you started Edit!, the Create/Edit Screen has nothing on it except for the menu, Insert/Overwrite Indicator, and Cursor

Position Indicator at the bottom.

If you have already created or edited another document in the same work session, that document appears on the Create/Edit Screen. Unless this is the document you want to edit, you must clear the screen. First press [F3] to save the old document, if you haven't done so already. Then press [ESCAPE] to display the Main Menu. Select the **Change files** option by pressing [F10]. See the section Changing Document Files later in this manual for further instructions on using this option.

Retrieving a Document

To retrieve a document stored on a disk, press [SHIFT]-[F3] to select **Read in paper** from the Create/Edit Menu. Edit! then prompts you for the name of the document.

Next, type the document name and press [ENTER], or press [ENTER] without typing anything to edit the default document WORK.EDT. If the document you want is in a directory other than the current directory, type the directory name, the symbol \, and the document name. If the document is stored on a different disk from the disk containing the current directory, start by typing the letter that designates the disk drive.

For example, suppose you want to edit a paper called SYMBOLS that is in a floppy disk in drive A, but the current directory is C:\PAPERS. To edit this document, respond to the document name prompt by typing **A:\SYMBOLS** and pressing [ENTER]. When you press [ENTER], Edit! displays the document on the Create/Edit Document Screen.

NOTE: If you created the document with other word processing software and did not follow the Edit! spacing rules, parts of the document may be missing. If this happens, exit from Edit! **WITHOUT SAVING THE DOCUMENT.** Then use the other software to correct the spacing problems before attempting to work on the document with Edit! again.

USER'S GUIDE 19

Saving Your Work

As you edit a document, press [F3] to select **Save** every few minutes. Then you won't lose all your work if the computer is turned off for some reason; you'll lose only what you've done since the last time you used the **Save** option.

When you press [F3], Edit! prompts you for the name of the document file where you want to save your work. The name you typed when you used the **Read in paper** option is the default name. To save the document under a different name, type the new name and press [ENTER]. To save the document under the default name, press [ENTER] without typing anything. By using a different name, you can retain the original, unedited version of the document. When you press [ENTER], Edit! records your work on the disk and returns you to where you left off, so you can resume editing.

Other Create/Edit Menu Options

To check the document for problems with words, sentences, paragraphs, or overall structure, select **Check**. See the Checking a Document section later in this manual for instructions on using this option.

Use the **Reformat** option to adjust line lengths if inserting or deleting text has left some lines too long or too short. To adjust a long or short line as well as the remainder of the paragraph, move the cursor to the start of the line and press [F7].

For instructions on using the **Recheck** option, see the next section of this manual, Checking a Document. Use **Recheck** only if you have interrupted the checking feature temporarily to make a change in a document.

With the **Find** option, you can search for a word or group of characters from the cursor location to the end of the document. When you press [F9] to select **Find,** Edit! prompts you to enter the text you want to find. Type the text exactly as it is in the document, then press [ENTER].

Edit! highlights the first text in the document that matches what you typed. To find the next place where the same text appears, press [F9] and [ENTER].

To review the pre-write screens, including what you typed on Pre-Write Screen 5, press [SHIFT]-[F4]. After reviewing the screens, press [ESCAPE] to return to the document.

For information about how to use the keyboard with Edit!, press [F1]. To list the checking levels and the kinds of checks you can make on each level, press [F2].

To return to the Main Menu, press [ESCAPE].

CHECKING A DOCUMENT

To check a document, select **Edit** from the Main Menu and retrieve the document if it is not already on the screen. See the Editing a Document section earlier in this manual for instructions on using the **Edit** option and retrieving a document.

```
      Edit is a computer editing program designed specifically to
be used in English writing classes, in the writing laboratory,
or on home computers.




















Word Level
Sentence Level
Paragraph Level
Overall paper level
Esc Create/Edit menu
F1    Help         F2 Tutorial
```

Figure 4 - Checking Menu

When the document you want to check appears on the screen, press [F4] to select **Check** from the Create/Edit Menu. Edit! first checks the spacing before paragraphs and at the ends of sentences. Each paragraph must be indented four spaces, and each punctuation mark at the end of a sentence must be followed by two spaces, or the checking feature won't work properly. If Edit! doesn't find a correctly indented paragraph near the start of the docu-

USER'S GUIDE 21

ment, it displays a message telling you so. Then it displays the Checking Menu.

To check for punctuation errors, word confusion, slang, vagueness, wordiness, cliches, euphemisms, sexism, racism, or stuffiness, select the **Word level** option.

To check for sentences beginning with "It" and "There," agreement between verbs and subjects, passive voice, correct use of indefinite pronouns, sentence fragments, and sentences too long or too short, select **Sentence level**.

To check for smooth transitions between paragraphs, topic sentences and concluding sentences, and correct usage of indefinite pronouns, select **Paragraph level**.

To check how fully you've developed your ideas in the document and whether its sentence lengths are varied enough for readability, select **Overall paper**. Also select this option to read the Edit! post-write screens, which help you to assess the effectiveness of your document, or to list statistics about your document such as the average number of words per paragraph.

You should usually make checks following the sequence in which they are listed on menus. In other words, check the document first at the word level, then at the paragraph level, and so on. See the headings that follow for instructions on using these checking options.

For information about using Edit! menus, press [F1].

To list the checking levels and the kinds of checks you make on each level, press [F2].

When you finish checking a document, press [ESCAPE] to return to the Create/Edit Menu.

Checking Words

At the word level, you can check for punctuation problems, words that are often confused with each other, slang and other questionable terminology, vagueness and wordiness, cliches and euphemisms, racism and sexism, and stuffiness.

To check a document at the word level, press **W** to se-

EDIT!

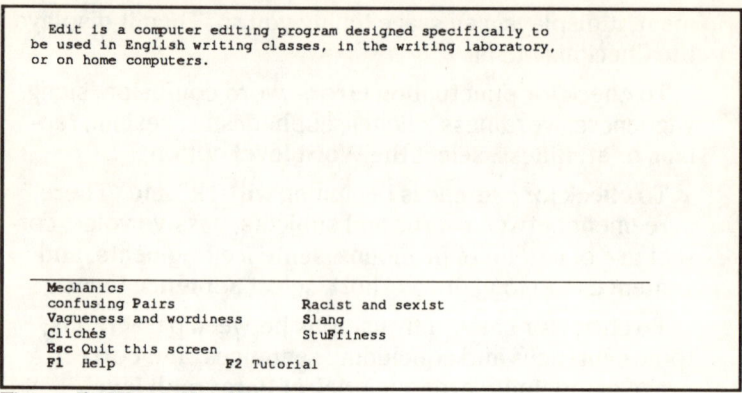

Figure 5 - Word Checking Menu

lect **Word level** from the Checking Menu. Edit displays the Word Checking Menu.

To check for punctuation and capitalization errors, press **M** to select the **Mechanics** option from the Word Checking Menu. To look for words often confused with each other, such as "stationary" and "stationery," press **P** to select **Confusing pairs**. To check for vague, wordy, or lifeless expressions, press **V** to select **Vagueness and wordiness.** To search out language that may convey prejudice against minority groups or women, press **R** to select **Racism and sexism**. To check for trite expressions and euphemisms, press **C** to select **Cliches**. To look for inappropriate informal language, press **S** to select **Slang**. To look for pompous language and jargon, press **F** to select **Stuffiness.**

For information about using Edit! menus, press F1 . To list the checking levels and the kinds of checks you can make on each level, press F2 . When you finish checking words, press ESCAPE to return to the Checking Menu. When you select a word checking option, Edit! begins checking the document.

If Edit! doesn't find a possible problem, it displays a message telling you that it has completed the check. Press **Space** to display the Word Checking Menu again.

If Edit! does find a possible problem, it highlights the problem. If there is a message explaining this specific

USER'S GUIDE 23

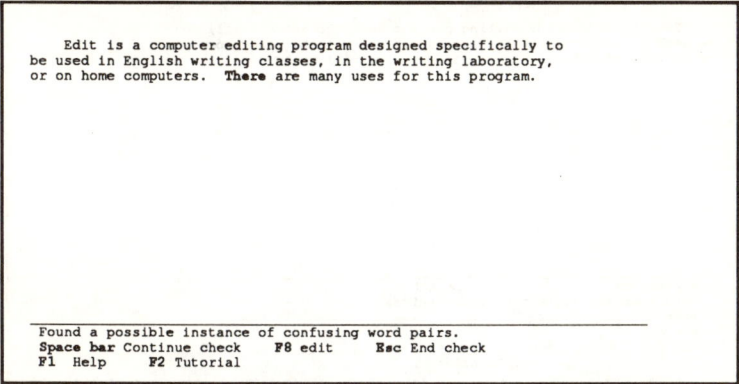

Figure 6 - Editing/Checking Menu

problem, it is displayed first. To clear the message from the screen, press **Space**. Edit! then displays the Checking Menu.

You can use the items on this menu to correct or ignore a possible problem that Edit! has pointed out. For example, during a check for word confusion, Edit! highlights the words "there" and "their" if it finds them, because people frequently type one of these words when they mean the other. When Edit! highlights a "there" that you used correctly, press the space bar to remove the highlighting and go on looking for other possible problems. If you meant to type "their" instead, press F8, type "their" in place of "there," and press F8 again to resume the check for confusing word pairs.

To display helpful information about using Edit! menus, press F1. For tutorial information about the writing problem for which you are checking, press F2. For example, if you press this key after selecting **Confusing Pairs** from the Word Checking Menu, you see information about words that are often confused with each other.

To return to the Word Checking Menu, press ESCAPE.

Checking Sentences

At the sentence level, you can check for sentences beginning with the expletives "It" and "There." You can also

```
┌─────────────────────────────────────────────────────────────────┐
│   Edit is a computer editing program designed specifically to   │
│   be used in English writing classes, in the writing laboratory,│
│   or on home computers.  There are many uses for this program.  │
│                                                                 │
│                                                                 │
│                                                                 │
│                                                                 │
│   ─────────────────────────────────────────────────────────────│
│   Expletives              Length                                │
│   Verb Analysis (agreement and passives)                        │
│   Indefinite pronouns                                           │
│   Fragment                                                      │
│   Esc Quit this screen                                          │
│   F1  Help              F2 Tutorial                             │
└─────────────────────────────────────────────────────────────────┘
```

Figure 7 - Sentence Checking Menu

check for agreement between subjects and verbs, correct use of indefinite pronouns, incomplete sentences, and sentences that are too long or too short.

To check a document at the sentence level, press **S** to select **Sentence** from the Checking Menu. Edit! displays the Sentence Checking Menu.

To check for sentences that begin with "It" and "There," select the **Expletives** option. For a listing that shows the number of words in each sentence, select **Length.** To check for subject-verb agreement and passive voice, press **V** to select **Verb analysis.** To check for correct use of indefinite pronouns such as "other" and "each," press **I** to select **Indefinite pronouns.** To check for sentence fragments, press **F** to select **Fragments.** Instructions for using each of these options appear later in this section of the manual.

For information about using Edit! menus, press [F1]. To list the kinds of checking Edit! can do, press [F2].

When you finish checking sentences, press [ESCAPE] to return to the Checking Menu.

Checking for Expletives

To check for sentences beginning with "It" and "There," press **E** to select **Expletives** from the Sentence Checking Menu.

If Edit! doesn't find any possible expletives, it displays a message telling you that it has completed the check. Press the space bar to display the Sentence Checking Menu again.

If Edit! does find a sentence beginning with "It" or "There," it highlights the word and displays a message pointing out the problem. It also displays the Editing/Checking Menu, which is illustrated earlier in this section. You can use options on this menu to edit the sentence and eliminate the expletive or to ignore it. To leave the expletive unchanged and continue checking for others, press the space bar. To edit the sentence and eliminate the expletive, press [F8], rewrite the sentence, then press [F8] again to resume the check for expletives.

For information about using Edit! menus, press [F1]. For tutorial information about expletives, press [F2]. To return to the Sentence Checking Menu, press [ESCAPE].

Checking Sentence Length

To check for sentences that are too long or too short, press **L** to select **Length** from the Sentence Checking Menu. First, Edit! checks the spacing and punctuation to determine where sentences begin and end. It then displays the Sentence Length Screen.

This screen shows your document divided into sentences, with blank lines between them. If you have not in-

```
23 words     Edit is a computer editing program designed specifically to
             be used in English writing classes, in the writing
             laboratory, or on home computers.

7 words      There are many uses for this program.




                UpArrow Up 1 Sentence  DnArrow Down 1 Sentence  PgUp Up 5 PgDn Down 5
                F1 Help  F2 Tutorial   F8 Edit    Esc Previous menu
```

Figure 8 - Sentence Length Screen

dented each paragraph four spaces and included two spaces after the punctuation mark at the end of each sentence, Edit! cannot separate the sentences properly.

Along the left side of the Sentence Length Screen, Edit! lists the length of each sentence. If a sentence includes more than 24 words, Edit! adds an "l" after the word count to indicate that the sentence may be too long. For a sentence with fewer than four words, Edit! adds an "s" after the word count to indicate that it may be too short.

To move the display down by one sentence press the down arrow key (↓), and to move it down five sentences press PAGE DOWN.

To move the display up by one sentence press the up arrow key (↑), and to move it up five sentences at a time, press PAGE UP.

To leave the checking feature temporarily so you can rewrite a sentence, press F8. When you finish, press this key again to return to the Sentence Length Screen and see the new word count.

For help with using Edit! menus, press F1. For tutorial information about sentence lengths, press F2. To return to the Sentence Checking Menu, press ESCAPE.

Analyzing Verbs

To check for subject-verb agreement and passive voice, press **V** to select **Verb analysis** from the Sentence Check-

```
        Edit is a computer editing program designed specifically to
be used in English writing classes, in the writing laboratory,
or on home computers.  There are many uses for this program.




















Arrow keys move cursor Begin   End   Skip   Unmark  Analyze
F1   Help    F2 Tutorial  Esc Sent. Check.  Menu
```

Figure 9 - Verb Analysis Menu

USER'S GUIDE

ing Menu. Edit! displays the Verb Analysis Menu. While the Verb Analysis Menu is displayed you cannot change the text, but all the keys that move the cursor (right arrow, left arrow, page down, etc.) work as they do when the Editing Menu is displayed.

You must mark each verb before Edit! can analyze it. To mark a verb:

1. Use the arrow keys to move the cursor to the verb's first letter.

2. Press **B** to select **Begin** from the menu. If the verb has two parts that are separated, as in the phrase "has not yet begun," go to Step 3. Otherwise, go on to Step 7.

3. Move the cursor to the space or punctuation mark after the verb.

4. Press **S** to select **Skip to next part** from the menu.

5. Move the cursor to the beginning of the next part of the verb. For example, in the phrase "has not yet begun," you would move the cursor to the b in "begun."

6. Press **B** to select **Begin** again.

7. Move the cursor to the space or punctuation mark after the verb.

8. Press **E** to select **End marking** from the menu. Edit! highlights the verb you have marked.

9. Press **A** to select **Analyze** from the menu.

```
      Edit is a computer editing program designed specifically to
be used in English writing classes, in the writing laboratory,
or on home computers.  There are many uses for this program.




















   is marked as verb.
   Record    Forget    F8 Edit    F1 Help    F2 Tutorial    Esc Verb Marking Menu
```

Figure 10 - Marked Verb Menu

Edit! displays a message telling you if the verb you are analyzing seems to be singular, plural, passive, or incorrect. To clear this message from the screen, press the space bar. If Edit! cannot identify the verb as singular, plural, or passive, or if you clear the message from the screen, you see a message confirming that you have marked the verb. Below this message is the Marked Verb Menu.

If the verb you have marked is the main verb in the sentence, press **R** to record it. This helps Edit! to sort out complete sentences from sentence fragments when you use the **Fragments** option from the Sentence Checking Menu later on. If the verb is not the main verb in the sentence, press **F** to select the **Forget** option from the Marked Verb Menu.

To suspend the verb analysis temporarily so you can edit the verb you have marked, press [F8]. When you finish editing, press it again to return to the Verb Analysis Menu.

If you change your mind about analyzing or marking a verb you have highlighted, press **U** to select **Unmark** from the Verb Analysis Menu.

For help with marking and analyzing verbs, press [F1]. To display tutorial information about subject-verb agreement, press [F2].

To return to the Sentence Checking Menu, press [ESCAPE].

Checking Indefinite Pronouns

To check for correct use of indefinite pronouns such as "all" and "other," press **I** to select **Indefinite pronouns** from the Sentence Checking Menu. Edit! begins checking the document.

If Edit! doesn't find any indefinite pronouns, it displays a message telling you that it has completed the check. Press the space bar to display the Sentence Checking Menu again.

If Edit! does find an indefinite pronoun, it highlights the pronoun and displays an message about it at the bottom of the screen. To clear the message from the screen, press the space bar. Edit! then displays the Editing/Checking Menu.

USER'S GUIDE 29

To correct an error in the pronoun's usage, press [F8] to leave the checking feature temporarily. When you finish correcting the error, press it again to resume checking. If a highlighted pronoun is used correctly, press the space bar to remove the highlighting and go on looking for indefinite pronouns.

For information about using Edit! menus, press [F1]. To display the tutorial about indefinite pronouns, press [F2]. To return to the Sentence Checking Menu, press [ESCAPE].

Checking for Sentence Fragments

To check for incomplete sentences, press **F** to select **Fragments** from the Sentence Checking Menu. Edit! displays the Sentence Fragment Screen.

```
OK  Edit is a computer editing program designed specifically to be used in
    English writing classes, in the writing laboratory, or on home computers.
OK  There are many uses for this program.




















    UpArrow Up 1 Sentence   DnArrow Down 1 Sentence   PgUp Up 5   PgDn Down 5
    F1 Help   F2 Tutorial   F8 Edit   Esc Previous menu
```

Figure 11 - Sentence Fragment Screen

This screen shows the document divided into sentences. If the paragraphs in the document are not indented four spaces, or if two spaces don't follow the punctuation mark at the end of each sentence, Edit! cannot separate the sentences properly. To leave the checking feature temporarily so you can correct the spacing, press [F8]. When the spacing is correct, press it again to return to the Sentence Fragment Screen.

To the left of each sentence, Edit! displays a notation. The notation "Fr?", which stands for "Fragment?", marks sentences for which you have not marked a main verb. The notation "OK" indicates that you have marked a main verb and that, therefore, the sentence appears to be complete.

To move the display down by one sentence, press the down arrow key. To move the display down by five sentences, press [PAGE DOWN]. To move the display up one sentence, press the up arrow key. To move it up five sentences, press [PAGE UP].

To leave the checking feature temporarily and edit an incomplete sentence, press [F8]. When you finish editing, press it again to return to the Sentence Fragment Screen.

For information about using the Sentence Fragment Screen, press [F1]. For tutorial information about sentence fragments, press [F2]. To return to the Sentence Checking Menu, press [ESCAPE].

Checking Paragraphs

At the paragraph level, you can check for smooth transitions from one idea to another. You can also see that pronoun references are clear and correct. In addition, you can check each paragraph for topic and concluding sentences, and you can mark them to check the development of your ideas at the overall paper level later on.

To check a document at the paragraph level, press **P** to select **Paragraph level** from the Checking Menu. Edit! dis-

```
        Edit is a computer editing program designed specifically to
   be used in English writing classes, in the writing laboratory,
   or on home computers.  There are many uses for this program.




   Connecting phrases
   Pronoun referents
   Topic and concluding sentences
   F1  Help    F2  Tutorial    Esc  Checking Menu
```

Figure 12 - Paragraph Checking Menu

USER'S GUIDE 31

plays the Paragraph Checking Menu.

To check for words and phrases that provide transition from one idea to another, such as "therefore" and "as a result," select **Connecting phrases**. To see that pronouns' antecedents, or the nouns to which they refer, are clear and that the pronouns agree with them, select **Pronoun referents**. To mark topic and concluding sentences, select **Topic and concluding sentences**.

Instructions for using each of these options appear later in this section of the manual. For information about using Edit! menus, press F1.

To list the checking levels and the kinds of checking Edit! can do at each level, press F2.

Checking Transitions

To check for words and phrases that provide transition between ideas, press **C** to select **Connecting phrases** from the Paragraph Checking Menu. Edit! scans the document.

```
      Edit is a computer editing program designed specifically to
be used in English writing classes, in the writing laboratory,
or on home computers.  Therefore, there are many uses for this
program.




















Found a possible instance of transitions and connecting phrases.
Space bar Continue check    F8 edit      Esc End check
F1  Help      F2 Tutorial
```

Figure 13 - Paragraph Editing Menu

If Edit! doesn't find any transitions in the document, it displays a message telling you that the check for transitions is complete. Press the space bar to clear this message from the screen and display the Paragraph Checking Menu.

If Edit! does find a transition, it highlights that word or phrase. It also displays a message about the transition at the bottom of the screen. For example, if your document includes the phrase "as a result," Edit! highlights that phrase and displays the message, "Transition used to show cause and effect."

Reread the paragraph to see if the transition word or phrase is appropriate. For example, if you've used the phrase "as a result," make sure you've spelled out both the cause and the effect that it's intended to show. Then press the space bar to clear the message from the screen. Edit! displays the Checking/Editing Menu.

To leave the checking feature temporarily so you can change a transition or rewrite a sentence, press [F8]. When you finish, press it again to resume the check for transitions.

To remove the highlighting from the transition and continue the check, press the space bar.

For help with using Edit! menus, press [F1]. For tutorial information about transitions, press [F2]. To return to the Paragraph Checking Menu, press [ESCAPE].

Checking Pronouns

To check whether pronouns have clear antecedents and that the pronouns and antecedents agree, press **P** to select **Pronoun referents** from the Paragraph Menu.

If Edit! doesn't find any pronouns in the document, it displays a message telling you that the check for pronouns is complete. Press the space bar to clear this message from the screen and display the Paragraph Checking Menu.

If Edit! does find a pronoun, it highlights the pronoun. It also displays a message about the pronoun at the bottom of the screen. For example, if it finds the word "them," Edit! displays the message, "Plural; be sure the referent is plural." Look for the noun to which the pronoun refers, and determine whether the noun and the pronoun agree.

To change a pronoun or rewrite a sentence, press [F8] to leave the checking feature temporarily and return to the Create/Edit Menu. When you finish editing, press [F8] again to resume the check for pronouns.

To remove highlighting from the pronoun and continue the check without making a change, press the space bar.

USER'S GUIDE 33

For information on using Edit! menus, press [F1]. For tutorial information about pronoun referents, press [F2]. To return to the Paragraph Checking Menu, press [ESCAPE].

Marking Topic and Concluding Sentences

To check for topic and concluding sentences and mark them, press **T** to select Topic and Concluding sentences from the Paragraph Checking Menu. Edit! highlights the first sentence of the document and displays the Sentence Marking Menu.

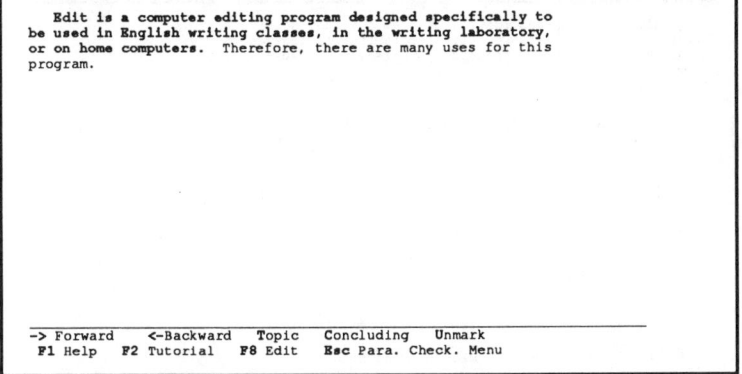

```
    Edit is a computer editing program designed specifically to
    be used in English writing classes, in the writing laboratory,
    or on home computers.  Therefore, there are many uses for this
    program.




















-> Forward    <-Backward    Topic     Concluding    Unmark
F1 Help       F2 Tutorial   F8 Edit   Esc Para. Check. Menu
```
Figure 14 - Sentence Marking Menu

To mark a highlighted sentence as a topic sentence of the paragraph, press **T**. To mark a highlighted sentence as a concluding sentence of a paragraph, press **C**.

To highlight another sentence, press the right or left arrow keys.

To remove the marking from a sentence if you decide it isn't a topic or concluding sentence after all, position the cursor on the sentence and press **U**.

Edit! doesn't recognize sentences that don't have two spaces after their final punctuation marks, and it may combine them with other sentences. To leave checking temporarily to correct the spacing, press [F8]. When you finish, press it again to resume marking sentences.

For help on how to mark sentences, press [F1]. For tutorial information about topic and concluding sentences, press F2. To return to the Paragraph Checking Menu, press ESCAPE.

Checking an Overall Document

At the overall paper level, you can check to see that you have fully developed the ideas you set forth in a document, and that you have used sentences of varying lengths to avoid monotony.

```
     Edit is a computer editing program designed specifically to
be used in English writing classes, in the writing laboratory,
or on home computers.  Therefore, there are many uses for this
program.




















Variety
Development
Post-write
Statistics
F1 Help     F2 Tutorial    Esc Checking Menu
```

Figure 15 - Overall Paper Checking Menu

You can also list statistics about the document, such as the average number of words per paragraph, and you can read the Edit! post-write screens for help in assessing the document's effectiveness.

To check an overall document, press **O** to select **Overall paper** from the Checking Menu. Edit! displays the Overall Paper Checking Menu.

To check whether you have varied the sentence lengths, select the **Variety** option. To check whether you have developed the ideas in the document sufficiently, select **Development**. To read the Edit! post-write screens, select **Post-write**. To list facts about a document such as the numbers of words, sentences and paragraphs, select **Statistics.** Instructions for using each of these options appear later in this section of the manual.

For information on how to use Edit! menus, press

[F1]. To list the Edit! checking levels and the kinds of checks you can make at each level, press [F2].

To return to the Checking Menu when you finish checking the overall document, press [ESCAPE].

Checking Sentence Length Variety

To check the variety of sentence lengths, press **V** to select **Variety** from the Overall Paper Checking Menu. Edit! displays the Sentence Length Variety Screen. This screen shows your document divided into paragraphs and sentences. On the left, the sentences are numbered: S1 for the first sentence in a paragraph, S2 for the second, and so forth.

```
S  1:   23 wds  Edit is a computer editing program designed specifically to
                be used in English writing classes, in the writing
                laboratory, or on home computers.
S  2:    8 wds  Therefore, there are many uses for this program.




              UpArrow Up 1 Sentence  DnArrow Down 1 Sentence  PgUp Up 5  PgDn Down 5
              F1   Help   F2 Tutorial   F8 Edit     Esc Previous menu
```
Figure 16 - Sentence Length Variety Screen

If you have not indented each paragraph four spaces and included two spaces after the punctuation mark at the end of each sentence, Edit! cannot separate the sentences properly. To leave the checking feature temporarily and correct the spacing, press [F8]. When you finish making corrections, press [F8] to display the Sentence Length Variety Screen again. After each sentence number, Edit! shows how many words this sentence includes. Scan these word counts to see that the sentences vary in length.

To move the display down one sentence, press the down arrow key.

To move down five sentences, press [PAGE DOWN].

To move the display up one sentence press the up arrow key. To move up five sentences, press `PAGE UP`.

To leave the checking feature temporarily so you can rewrite a sentence, press `F8`. Press it again when you finish to return to the Sentence Length Variety Screen.

For help with using the Sentence Length Variety Screen, press `F1`. For tutorial information about sentence lengths, press `F2`. To return to the Overall Paper Checking Menu, press `ESCAPE`.

Checking Idea Development

Before you can use the **Development** option from the Overall Paper Menu, you *must* mark the topic and concluding sentences of each paragraph in the document. Otherwise, Edit! will not display the document correctly and may not function properly.

Turn to the Checking Paragraphs heading earlier in this section of the manual for instructions on marking topic and concluding sentences.

```
                ──────── Paragraph   1 ────────
    Topic       -Edit is a computer editing program designed specifically to
                 be used in English writing classes, in the writing
                 laboratory, or on home computers.
    Concluding  -Therefore, there are many uses for this program.











    UpArrow  Up 1 Sentence    DnArrow  Down 1 Sentence    PgUp  Up 5  PgDn  Down 5
    F1  Help   F2  Tutorial    F8 Edit      Esc Previous menu
```

Figure 17 - Development Screen

To select **Development**, press D. Edit! displays the Development Screen.

This screen shows the topic and concluding sentences that you marked for each paragraph. To move the display down one sentence, press the down arrow key. To move down five sentences, press `PAGE DOWN`. To move the display up one sentence, press the up arrow key. To move up five sentences, press [PAGE UP].

To leave the checking feature temporarily so you can view or rewrite a paragraph, press [F8]. Then press it again to return to the Development Screen.

For information about how to use the Development Screen, press [F1]. For tutorial information about developing your ideas in a document, press [F2]. To return to the Overall Paper Checking Menu, press [ESCAPE].

The Post-Write Screens

To read the Edit! post-write screens, which can help you to determine whether your document needs further work, press **P** to select the **Post-write** option from the Overall Paper Checking Menu. Edit! displays the first of the three screens.

The first and second post-write screens list a total of ten questions to help you make sure the document achieves its purpose. The third screen shows the information you entered on Pre-Write Screen 5 about the document's audience, main idea, purpose, format, and tone.

Press [PAGE DOWN] to go from one post-write screen to the next. Press [PAGE UP] to go to the previous post-write screen.

For information about moving from one post-write screen to another, press [F1]. For a list of the checking levels and the items you can check at each level, press [F2].

Press [ESCAPE] to return to the Overall Paper Checking Menu.

Displaying Statistics

To list the average number of words per paragraph and other statistics about your document, press **S** to select **Statistics** from the Overall Paper Checking Menu. Edit! lists the:

- number of words, sentences, and paragraphs in the document
- average words per sentence
- average sentences per paragraph
- average words per paragraph

The Overall Paper Checking Menu remains on the screen. When you finish reading the statistics, select another option.

SAVING A DOCUMENT ON A DISK

You can save a document you've worked on by pressing [F3] to select the **Save** option from either the Main Menu or the Create/Edit Menu. Save the document before you begin creating or editing another document, exit from Edit!, or turn off the computer. Otherwise, you will lose the work you've just done. Save the document now and then as you create or edit it, too.

When you press [F3], Edit! prompts you for the name of the file where you want to save your work. The name you typed when you began creating the document is the default name.

If you save the document under the default name, the latest version replaces the version without the changes you just made. Therefore, if you want to save both the revised version and the original, save the revised version under a different name.

- To save the document under a different name, type the new name and press [ENTER].

- To save it under the default name, press [ENTER] without typing anything.

Edit! continues to display the Create/Edit Screen with the document you just saved. When you resume editing, the cursor is where it was when you pressed [F3].

CHANGING DOCUMENT FILES

If you have been working on one document and want to edit another, you must clear the screen before you can retrieve the document for editing. Save the old document and then select the **Change files** option from the Main Menu. To select **Change files,** press [F10]. Edit! clears the old document from the screen and displays the Create/

Edit Menu. You can press [SHIFT]-[F3] to retrieve a document.

PRINTING A DOCUMENT

Before you can print a document, you must display it on the screen. If it isn't displayed already, clear the screen if necessary and then press [SHIFT]-[F3] from the Edit/Create screen to retrieve it.

With the document on the screen, press [ESCAPE] to return to the Main Menu and then press **P** to select **Print**. Edit! displays a message asking if you are ready to begin printing. Make sure your printer is turned on and loaded with paper. When the printer is ready, press **Y**. (If you change your mind about printing, press **N** instead.)

If you have typed information on Pre-Write Screen 5, Edit! asks if you want to print that information on a separate page. Type **N** if you do not want to print this information or **Y** if you do. Edit! then begins printing the document. To stop the printer before it finishes the document, press the space bar.

CHANGING THE DIRECTORY

Suppose you have been working with documents in one directory and you now want to edit several documents in another directory. Instead of typing the new directory name with each document name after you select **Edit** from the Main Menu, you can save time by designating the second directory as the current directory.

To change the current directory, press **D** to select **new Drive/Directory** from the Main Menu. Edit! then displays a message at the top of the screen that identifies the current directory and prompts you to name a new one.

Type the new directory name and press [ENTER]. If you decide not to change the current directory, press [ENTER] without typing anything.

If you enter a new directory name, Edit! displays a new message at the top of the screen to identify the new directory.

Note that changing the current directory does not change the default directory. That is, the next time you use Edit!, it will save your documents in the default directory unless you again name a different current directory. You can change the default directory, however, by using the **Setup** option from the Main Menu. See the Changing the Edit! Setup section below for instructions.

RETURNING TEMPORARILY TO DOS

If your computer has enough memory, you can carry out DOS functions such as copying a document file or listing the contents of a directory while still working in Edit! Press **O** to select **DOS command** from the Main Menu.

When you select **DOS command**, a DOS prompt appears on the screen. You can now use DOS commands such as COPY and TYPE.

Remember that you are in the directory where you were working in Edit! For example, suppose you were working with a document in the C:\PAPERS directory. If you select **DOS command** and type `dir` and press [ENTER] at the DOS prompt, DOS lists the files in the directory C:\PAPERS.

To return to Edit! when you finish with DOS, type `exit` at the DOS prompt and press [ENTER]. Edit! displays the Main Menu.

CHANGING THE EDIT! SETUP

The Edit! setup determines:
- the colors that appear on the screen
- the type of printer to be used with Edit!
- the directory where Edit! saves and retrieves documents if no other directory is specified
- the right margin of documents

To change the Edit! setup, press **S** to select **Setup** from the Main Menu. Edit! displays the Setup Menu.

To change the display color on a color monitor, select

USER'S GUIDE 41

Colors. To change the default directory where Edit! stores documents, select **Directory.** To reset the right margin, select Margin. To choose between the printer types you can use with Edit!, select Printer. Instructions for using these options appear later in this section.

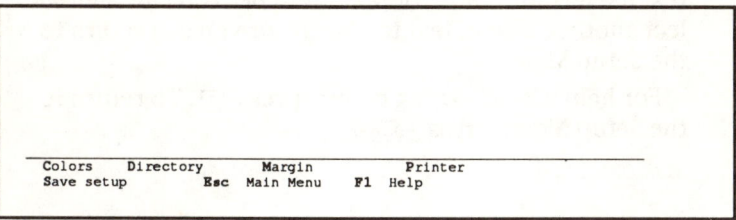

```
Colors     Directory      Margin            Printer
Save setup           Esc  Main Menu    F1   Help
```

Figure 18 - Setup Menu

To record the setup changes on the Edit! disk, press **S** to select **Save setup.** After saving the setup, Edit! continues to display the Setup Menu. For help using the **Setup** option, press F1.

To return to the Main Menu, press ESCAPE.

Changing Colors

On a color monitor, Edit! uses background and foreground colors to display normal text as well as bold text, underlined text, and highlighted, or reverse video, text. For any of these kinds of text, you can change the background color, the foreground color, or both.

To change the screen colors, press **C** to select **Colors** from the Setup Menu. Edit! displays the Color Setup Screen, which shows the color schemes for normal text, reverse video, bright (or bold) text, and underlined text. The Color Setup Menu appears at the bottom of the screen.

To change the color scheme for normal text, press **N.** For reverse video, press **R.** For bright text, press **B.** For underlined text, press **U.**

After selecting the kind of text for which you want to choose colors, press the up or down arrow until you see the background color you want to use. Some of the backgrounds blink. If you do not want a blinking background, keep pressing the arrow key until the color you want appears without the blinking.

Next, press the right or left arrow repeatedly until the text itself is the color you want it to be. You can then select another kind of text to change, or you can return to the Setup Menu.

For help with choosing colors, press [F1]. To return to the Setup Menu, press [ESCAPE].

Changing the Default Directory

To change the directory where Edit! saves and looks for documents if you don't specify another directory, press **D** to select **Directory** from the Setup Menu. Edit! displays a message at the top of the screen that identifies the default directory. At the bottom of the screen is the Default Directory Menu.

```
The default document directory is: default




Change default directory      Esc  Setup Menu
```

Figure 19 - Default Directory Menu

To designate a new default directory, press **C**. Edit! displays a prompt asking for the name of the new disk drive and directory. Type the disk drive and directory names and press [ENTER]. For example, to designate the papers directory on disk drive C as the new default, type `c:\papers` and press [ENTER]. The message at the top of the screen changes to show the new default directory.

To return to the Setup Menu, press [ESCAPE].

Resetting the Right Margin

To reset the right margin of a document, press **M** to select **Margin** from the Setup Menu. Edit! displays a message at the bottom of the screen that tells you the current right margin setting and asks what you want the new setting to be.

Type the new margin setting and press [ENTER]. To leave the margin setting unchanged, press [ENTER] without typing anything. Edit! displays the Setup Menu again. When you go to the Create/Edit Screen and display a document, you will see how the new setting affects the document.

The new margin setting stays in effect for all documents you work with in this Edit! session unless you change it again. However, unless you save the changes you have made in the new Edit! setup, the margin returns to its original setting the next time you use Edit!

Choosing a Printer

To set up Edit! to work with the kind of printer your computer uses, press **P** to select **Printer** from the Setup Menu. Edit! displays the printer options.

```
Printer Options

1    Epson compatible
2    HP LaserJet compatible
3    HP ThinkJet
4    IBM Proprinter
5    NEC Pinwriter
6    C. Itoh F10-40/55

0    Setup Menu

Printer is now set to Epson compatible.

To select a different printer, type its number and press CR.
To return to the Setup Menu, type 0 and press CR.
```

Figure 20 - Printer Options Menu

If your computer uses one of the printers listed, press the key for the number of that printer, then press [ENTER]. Otherwise, try the default selection, Epson-compatible. Next, press **0** and [ENTER] to return to the Setup Menu.

NOTES: To determine whether a printer is Epson-compatible, check the printer's technical manual. If your printer does not work correctly with the Edit! printer option you have chosen, try others until you find the one that works best.

Saving Changes in the Edit! Setup

To save the changes you have made in the Edit! setup so that it uses them for future work sessions as well as the current one, press **S** to select **Save setup** from the Setup Menu. Edit! records the changes and continues to display the Setup Menu.

NOTE: Before you attempt to save a new setup, be sure there is no write-protect tab on the Edit! program disk.

QUITTING EDIT!

To stop using Edit!, press **Q** to select **Quit** from the Main Menu. Edit! displays a message telling you whether you have changed the document since you last saved it. If you haven't changed the document, you can press:

• [ESCAPE] to return to the Main Menu and continue editing the document.

• [F4] to exit from Edit and return to DOS.

If you have changed the document since you last saved it, you can press:

• [F3] to save the document and continue editing it.

• [F4] to save your latest work, exit from Edit!, and return to DOS.

• [X] to exit from Edit! and return to DOS without saving your latest work.

• [ESCAPE] to resume editing without saving your latest changes.